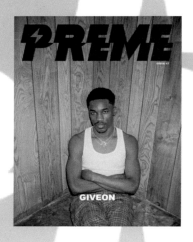

GIVEON

MARIAH THE SCIENTIST

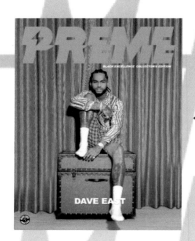

DAVE EAST

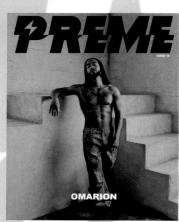

OMARION

JACK HARLOW

KAASH PAIGE

PAST ISSUES OF OUR MAGAZINE
COLLECT ALL NOW

SUBSCRIPTION

$15.00 EACH MONTH

Please Email Us at Prememag@gmail.com

Subscription includes 4 Random issues each year starting in 2021 a PREME tote as well as a 30% discount in our online store and priority access to all PREME events.

This subscription renews each month. You can choose start your subscription with our current issue or PREME

For every subscription we receive, PREME makes a $5 donation to Black Lives Matter initiatives, via blacklives.help.

Thank you for your support, and we hope you enjoy the magazine.

PREME
MAGAZINE

PREME is an independent black-owned magazine published monthly.

Our content focuses on emerging trends within entertainment, music, and pop culture.

Our mission is to empower creators and help them bridge gaps in their careers by giving them a platform to express themselves, their values, and creative goals.

The PREME issue consists of 3 to 4 covers a month, in both print and digital formats, giving our viewers a chance to stay tuned with their favorite artists but also keep discovering new influencers.

independent black owned

founder - creative director
anthony "supreme" thompson

fashion editors
raeana anais
maz

head of content
anthony "supreme" thompson

lead designer
tiffany tran

social media director
anthony "supreme" thompson

editor
noor kalouti

publicist
keisha - Lours
austin

ad
jason filler

creative directors
anthony supreme thompson

contributor writers

gregory gagliardi
tiffany bullock
Malcolm Trapp
starr savoy
tyler green
Sam Hadelman
guadalupe abigail ceja
Malik Peay
Gregory Castle
Thandie Sibanda
Amira Lawson
gabby felipe
Cydney Lee

contributing directors

darrin bush
tré loren
anthony supreme
70mm
jaminh
raeshon roberson
scout lazer
12am

contributing photographers

alex harper
diego palomino
amber asaly
anthony supreme
mariah winter
liz bretz
12am
steven moran
mia vasquez
antonie fougere
lamont roberson ii
amelia
david katzinger
stevie love
nicolita
dev dooley
faris
lanscine janneh
maddie córdoba
alan villlanueva
devin l'amoreaux
bri
coughs
dow studios
gunnerstal
breyona holt
Vante
cam kirk

contributing stylists

maz
raeana anais
vosi
martin tordby
kasuna kitara
triple joint
noah wallace
paco lampecinado
ani

contributing mua + hair teams

alero
lakeisha dale
lanii doa

#prememagazine - preme.xyz

index

COI LERAY
COI LERAY
COI LERAY
COI LERAY
COI LERAY
COI LERAY
COI LERAY

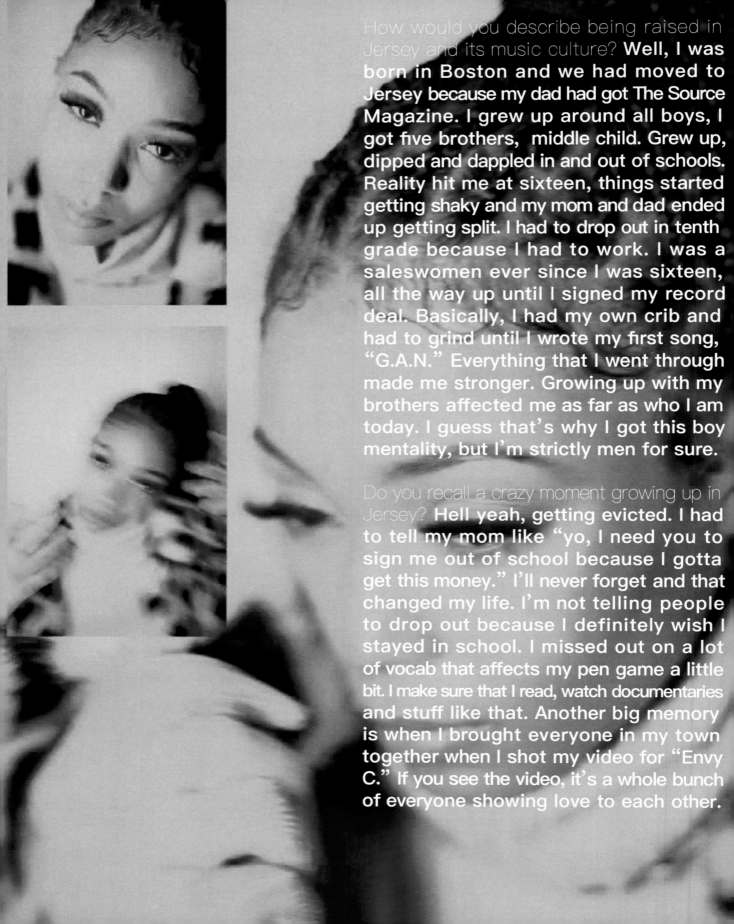

How would you describe being raised in Jersey and its music culture? Well, I was born in Boston and we had moved to Jersey because my dad had got The Source Magazine. I grew up around all boys, I got five brothers, middle child. Grew up, dipped and dappled in and out of schools. Reality hit me at sixteen, things started getting shaky and my mom and dad ended up getting split. I had to drop out in tenth grade because I had to work. I was a saleswomen ever since I was sixteen, all the way up until I signed my record deal. Basically, I had my own crib and had to grind until I wrote my first song, "G.A.N." Everything that I went through made me stronger. Growing up with my brothers affected me as far as who I am today. I guess that's why I got this boy mentality, but I'm strictly men for sure.

Do you recall a crazy moment growing up in Jersey? Hell yeah, getting evicted. I had to tell my mom like "yo, I need you to sign me out of school because I gotta get this money." I'll never forget and that changed my life. I'm not telling people to drop out because I definitely wish I stayed in school. I missed out on a lot of vocab that affects my pen game a little bit. I make sure that I read, watch documentaries and stuff like that. Another big memory is when I brought everyone in my town together when I shot my video for "Envy C." If you see the video, it's a whole bunch of everyone showing love to each other.

Women such as yourself as well as Megan Thee Stallion, City Girls, Rico Nasty, and more are starting to dominate hip-hop, what can you say about that? **I feel like women are going hard and doing shit a lot of men can't do. As you can see, women are getting a lot more recognition than before. For example, you got Cardi B and Megan Thee Stallion hitting all these numbers and doing all these viral things. Kylie Jenner hitting Forbes, even though she's not an artist, but she has a big influence when it comes to females. I know she influenced me. I just feel like women, we got that shit in the bag.**

Obviously, your father (Benzino) is a prominent figure in not only the music industry, but television as well. Is there any advice or contributions from Benzino that helped you grow and develop as an artist? **He just told me you can't fold in this business. It's going to get hard and there will be a lot of people trying to come at you. There will be a lot of mixed emotions and opinions, but you just gotta make sure you stand ten toes.**

Do you ever look back at some of the songs you recorded in your teenage years such as "Rock Back" or "Bow Down." If so, what do you think about those songs now? **Those were play times! I was young with my dad and we would visit him on vacation. He had this studio and I was like, "I'm about to make music." At that time, he wanted me to be a little princess so I couldn't really express how I really felt. So I put down the mic and just said "I'm going to be a doctor or something."**

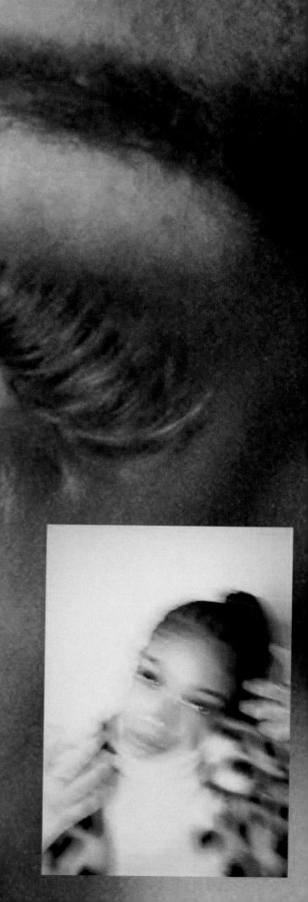

Your highly-acclaimed debut project 'EverythingCoZ' dropped in 2019, where were you at in life when you recorded that project? **I released it right before I got signed. Everything happened with me and my team. That was baby Coi though, when I drop my next project you'll see the growth.**

Fast forward to this year, you followed it up with 'EC2.' Which one did you have more fun creating and why? **A lot of those songs were actually recording the same time as my first project. One thing I can say, it's so versatile but this new shit is different.**

I know you met with a lot of record labels before inking your current deal, what ultimately made you chose Republic Records over the others? **They offered that bag haha. No, honestly, I signed to them because Monte and Avery [Lipman] are the only people who've been there since their label started. I met with everyone from Epic to Sony to Warner and everybody who used to work there is somewhere else now. However, when you go to Republic Records, you know that they've been there since day one so they're really dedicated to their artists. Clearly they've been doing it very well because they got artists like Ariana Grandey, Jonas Brothers, OVO, Young Money, NAV, The Weekend. You know he made a good decision adding me to that roster.**

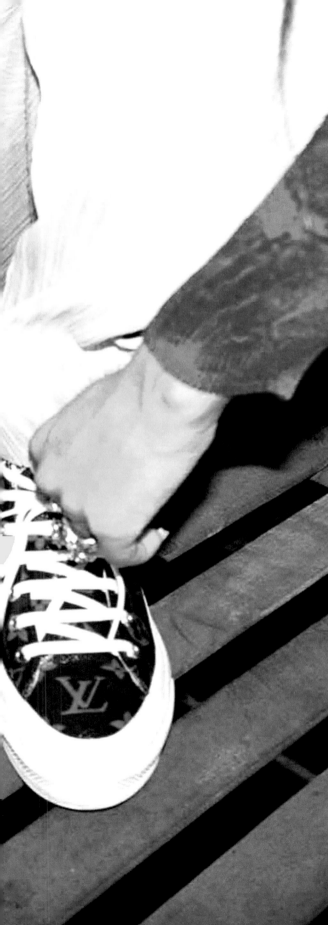

...ave some of the most ear-appealing ...s for your songs, what's the creative ...cess when it comes to making videos ...d songs? **I write through experience. This project is going to express a lot of trials and tribulations I went through. As far as me going through it with my team, my label, my ex, all kinds of stuff. The project is just going to be like damn, there's some turnt stuff to have people still shaking their ass.**

How about fashion, I feel like you're one of the best dressed artist to come out this decade. **I feel like fashion is all about the person wearing it. It's about swag, we have to bring that word back. It's all about the swag and how you own it or wear it. I feel like that's why a lot of people like my style. It's so aesthetic whether it me a size of men's Aemaris or me throwing on a tight ass dress to show them I'm sexy.**

Looking back on the past few months, what can say has had a major impact on your music? **The biggest change is me and this guy named Bobby Francis. He used to be Nipsey Hussle's mentor and he's been helping my manager out for a minute. Ever since he's came about, a lot of things have come to light. He's putting us on game and teaching us different things. It's just big to me because that was Nipsey's mentor. For him to just want to be involved in my growth, the dude is amazing. That's literally one of the biggest things to happen to me these past few months.**

This pandemic shocked the world in many ways. With the stay-at-home order issued in March , people had to find new ways to enjoy everyday activities. Athletes, especially, had to adapt and we saw this come to pass with the 2020 NBA bubble. But basketball wasn't the only competitive sport to be affected, BMX halted all racing events, team trips, and film productions. The pandemic left riders confused about what they should do next. San Diego BMX Champion, Chad Kerely, 26, was left confused how to stay consistent with his fans and sponsorships during the beginning of the pandemic. Kerely was forced to find new creative ways to do his job. Kerely decided to go back to his roots and begin freestyling and posting videos on Instagram from home. Sponsors started noticing that many riders took the same approach and came up with social media contests for BMXers.

PREME Magazine got the chance to catch up with Kerely as he prepared himself to film a part for his upcoming freestyle contest. We discussed his passion for BMX riding and his experience as Black BMX Rider in a predominantly white sport.

Growing up in San Diego, and started to ride at the age of four. How did your environment help you to become who you are now?

We're blessed enough, you know, here in San Diego with the weather that you can do it year-round. I got into BMX racing first, and my dad was super supportive and took me to all kinds of races. My mom was supportive, but she didn't travel as much with me; it was mainly my dad and me.
I started winning local races. I would win the district titles and state titles, and kind of from there, I branched out and started going to bigger races. And they put me in like this national age group bracket.
I feel like I got to experience it at a young age because I was so passionate about racing and being on my bike. I had to go out and train harder, and that kind of that whole process kind of burnt me out. By the time I was like 13 or 14 years old, I told my dad, "I can't do this anymore; this is too much." But it wasn't the fact that I didn't love riding. It was the kind of competitive aspect of it. Racing from start to finish every time, it was like, it was fun when you ride to practice, but the ultimate goal is to win races. And for me, I just wanted to ride my bike and have fun and enjoy that.
From 14 to 17, I was just going to the skate park damn near like every day and learning tricks and just playing on my bike. The whole thing around it is to have fun, express yourself, do freestyle, and just jump around. I really loved ultimately, riding bikes, jumping in the air, and that type of stuff. Which led me to where I'm now and just freestyle and just riding my bike for a living. It's a blessing for sure.

During the pandemic, Chad was able to continue building on his passion for freestyle riding, meanwhile sharing his content with the world. At the start of the pandemic he began to film bunny hops tricks around his house to create videos for his fans. Once the nation opened back up, Kerely took advantage of outdoor spots in San Diego that he'd never explored pre-Covid. Filming challenging breathtaking tricks, he was able to show his fan who he is. He showed his authenticity by using social media to showcase his style of riding, fashion, and music choice for his videos.

With Covid-19 cases still rising, how has the pandemic changed your life and how you work?

Once we figured out it's okay to kind of go outside, I started filming. In like, March I started filming for my new Rockstar energy like video part. In our sport, the most important thing to us, the most core thing, is to create a video that shows who you are. Because a contest just shows how good your tricks can be and under a certain amount of time, it doesn't really show your personality.

BMX began to come out with different events, but it was for social media. So you would film a video and have your fans vote for you. And then there is a judging panel, and they vote for you. I started entering those, which was a way to keep me active and in the contest scene. But for me, I just kind of took it as far as like, I can sit down and really do what I really want to just film every day.

COVID helped me focus on creating content rather than having contests blur the lines. Sometimes, when you travel, it takes so much energy and makes it hard to get in the filming mode. So this whole year I've just been in filming mode. It's been cool. I'm trying to stay active as far as these new events and contests that just pop up because of what's happening. So I just try to stay in the loop and then do what I can.

If the pandemic wasn't enough, in May George Floyd was murdered by the Minneapolis police officer — and Americans across the United States were outraged by yet another instance of police brutality against black men.

As I'm sure you saw, there were protests in several major cities and across the world. The murder of George Floyd shook our society to it's core. And during the wake of the protests, many companies and industries were challenged to stand with the Black Lives Matter movement. BMX did just that; affiliate brands and riders showed their solitary by making a statement and creating a change.

During the pandemic, a light was nationally shown on the struggles that African American's face everyday. How has the Black Lives Matter movement affected the bike industry?

In the riding industry, it did affect a lot of things. It stirred up a lot of stuff when it first came out. It was almost like people were pointing fingers at who had been racist in the past or might have done things, and things were just kind of opening up and like clearing out in the industry. Right now, it's on a stage for people to actually hear us. Now people can understand and be more open in the industry and understand what we might go through and how we might have to move just because of our skin color.

As a black BMX rider, Kerely has always dreamed about winning a gold medal at the X Games. Throughout his childhood, he grew up watching the X Games and had action figures of riders and ramps. In 2011, he received his first invite as an alternate rider. "It was like an unreal moment to even have an invite," Kerely says "and be around these other athletes and legends on this stage, with the people that I look up to competing against."Everything came full circle when he won first place at the 2013 X Games Los Angeles. His career took off after that and was able to land a major sponsorship with BMX affiliated companies.

Who did you look up to as a black boy wanting to get into BMX?

James Stewart was this other athlete that was so good. He was a huge inspiration in my career. When it came to racing, the style I was trying to obtain almost or like what I was inspired by was his demeanor on the dirt bike and being the best racer on the track. He was black and had gold goggles, and just the STEEZ was different. It was natural. The way he did it, you know, it just was tight. I had a pair, and I tried to put them on my helmet and just race around."

PORT OF SAN DIEGO

CRUISE SHIP TERMINAL

No Skateboarding

How are you helping to change the stigma around BMX in the black community?

Just following my passion and having fun and showing it now with social media. Black riders have a different style. It's just this automatic style that these other riders might not have. It just made me feel like there's a whole lane that there was for me, mostly because they had kind of paved the way for us. Now there are more black riders than ever, but it's still not really that many, but I mean, I think many black riders right now are shining. When I started riding, there were only a few pros to look up to and aspire to be like. Now it's really cool that I'm in a position to kind of inspire kids that are black and can relate to liking action sports. I know some people don't even know that BMX would even be an option. It shows that you can follow your passion and make something out of it if you just believe in yourself.

What advice would you give your younger self?

I would tell my younger self to enjoy the moments because I was always thinking of the next day or the next event that's happening. And it's hard to enjoy them. So now I find myself enjoying those little things.

What is next for Chad Kerely?

I'm getting married next year. So that's up next for sure. That's going to be in July of next year. So that's a big deal. I'm starting a whole new chapter of my life that I feel like I'm ready for, and I never thought I'd be ready for. I'm looking forward to tying the knot.

Next July, Kerely is getting married. So he's starting a whole new chapter in his life, one that he "never thought he'd be ready for" but actually is. BMX helped make him into the man he is today and that will never be taken for granted.

Brad Simms

Brad Simms, 33, was recently awarded not one but two prestigious awards. Winning the 2020 Nora Cup Rider Of The Year and 2020 Vital BMX Rider Of The Year means a great deal to him. Through his consistent effort to master all the tricks on his bike, Brad Simms created a name for himself of being one of the best bikers in the world.

As a Waldorf, MA native, being a black rider was not as popular in his hometown. Many couldn't understand his goal to become a BMX rider. Many would mock him by sneering "Oh, you are on that Tony Hawk stuff," recalls Simms. In Maryland, it was unheard of for a black kid to be so into biking; people saw it as an activity for the white kids. Being one the few black bikers at the skatepark didn't deter him from the sport. Continuing his journey allowed Simms to break his community's stigma through his dedication and passion for BMX.

PREME Magazine had the chance to sit down with the BMX superstar to discuss his achievements, life during the pandemic, and racial encounters in the sport.

How did you get introduced to riding?
My uncle introduced me to BMX when I was
11. My grandmother had 11 kids, my uncle
was one of the youngest and it wasn't a huge
age disparity. He would come over and
introduce me to riding. After that, I was kind
of never the same. I just started riding. And so
I just fell in love with the whole with the
freedom that came along with it.

**What was your experience growing up,
riding in Maryland?**
I didn't necessarily have any bad experiences
riding in Maryland. It was just, you know,
you're a kid, you kind of start out riding,
everything's fun, you're not really thinking
about any of the politics with it. The only thing
I really noticed growing up around BMX and
going to all the events was the lack of culture.
It wasn't multicultural growing up. I would go
to a little racetrack, and apart from my uncle
and me, we would be the only black BMX
riders there. So for years, I've just never really
thought it was a thing that black peoples did.
So it kind of felt slightly alienated. BMX is a
small community. Anytime you go ride around
Baltimore and usually, someone will say, "Oh,
you're doing that Tony Hawk stuff." It's not
usual. There is a disconnect.

Simms starts his day around 7:30 AM with
breakfast and stretching. After his morning
routine, he is ready to "pedal around the
streets" for a couple hours. He uses that time to
record thrilling new tricks for his Instagram.
After filming it is time to get down to business;
Simms meets with his team to discuss and
schedule upcoming projects, brand ideas, and
more.

How has your routine changed since the pandemic?

Not much has changed, like the whole pandemic hasn't really disrupted my routine. As if you've been in action sports, this is what you've been doing the majority of your career kind of just out just freestyling most of the time. I'm a bit more structured now. Simply because of new sponsors and stuff I have coming on board. This is the first time I've even been in a position where I've had to plan out my year. So this is kind of interesting.

What does winning the 2020 Nora Cup Rider and the 2020 Vital BMX Rider Of The Year mean to you?

That's a big one for me. Huge accolade. Because it's the only one I truly ever wanted to win, and it came to fruition. So I'm incredibly thankful. A lot of hard work, but it was something I've always wanted.

Having such a powerful platform, Simms feels he needs to speak up against racial discrimination in the BMX sport. "There's a lot of things you just grew up and learned to tolerate because you fear being a troublemaker." Simms says "If I speak up about this, what would happen?" Simms knows that if he becomes a political figure his sponsors might drop him as BMX athlete, because they judge him as controversial and unbefitting for the brand.

This is not unheard of; that is, companies sponsoring a black riders, actors or dancers, as a token instead of an appreciation of their technical or creative value.

During the pandemic the world got a close-up of the struggles that African Americans face every day. How have you experienced racial injustice during your time in BMX?

You have certain riders you want to come up and ask you like, "Hey, can I call you the N-word"! I'm and like, "No, you cannot. Why would I?" Just because your boy down the block gave you permission to call him, that doesn't mean I will. And for one, think about this, you're asking me permission to use a certain word around me. That should signal a red light to you.

What advice would you tell your younger self?

Plan. To learn how to plan/budget. You're going to be older, longer than you're going to be young. I'm really getting to stage one. I've never been in a position where I was able to plan.

Simms wants 2021 to be one of the best years yet; he plans to continue working hard with new sponsors and on new projects. The plan is to use digital platforms to reach a younger audience of athletes and empower them to choose BMX too, because basketball, football, and track are their not only options.

During the pandemic the world got a close-up of the struggles that African Americans face every day. How have you experienced racial injustice during your time in BMX?

You have certain riders you want to come up and ask you like, "Hey, can I call you the N-word"! I'm and like, "No, you cannot. Why would I?" Just because your boy down the block gave you permission to call him, that doesn't mean I will. And for one, think about this, you're asking me permission to use a certain word around me. That should signal a red light to you.

What advice would you tell your younger self?

Plan. To learn how to plan/budget. You're going to be older, longer than you're going to be young. I'm really getting to stage one. I've never been in a position where I was able to plan.

Simms wants 2021 to be one of the best years yet; he plans to continue working hard with new sponsors and on new projects. The plan is to use digital platforms to reach a younger audience of athletes and empower them to choose BMX too, because basketball, football, and track are their not only options.

• As an African American in the sport of BMX, have you experienced any discrimination or misconceptions?

Being African-American, I've definitely faced my fair share of misconceptions. Many of them are being expected to only ride the street. But I feel that there's been a shift, being that we have multiple media outlets/social platforms at the palm of our hands— people get to see a different side of us.

• What are some things you are doing within your community to engage young people with the sport and what are your future plans?

I try to remain low key but relatable in my community. Being that I live in a predominantly black/ brown neighborhood and that I'm the only professional BMX Rider it's important to me that my neighbors and their kids see that I am just like them.

I just chose an unconventional career, so when asked what I do for a living, most people in my community are completely caught off guard. They've never met someone that looks like them who rides BMX for a living. I believe they can see a little bit of themselves in me. I hope that that can help create the drive for them to also pursue their dreams.

As selfish as it sounds, it is fairly hard for me to share my future plans. I strongly believe that the more I share them, the more value they lose and it creates more expectations from others.

What is some advice you can give to the next generation of black BMX riders?

To any person of color that may read this, always strive to be the best you can be and push through the struggles no matter how hard they are! Your future self will thank you.

How do you distinguish yourself as an individual?

I personally feel that individuality is a natural thing. Accepting who I am is the most important part of that; we all learn and take from each other to build characteristics in ourselves that we want people to see but being our natural selves is something that will always stand out amongst everyone else.

• Walk us through a typical day for you?

Wake up, make my kids breakfast. Check social media then get dressed. I usually get out around 12. Hit up a few friends in the group chat and link with them in the city. When I'm done I head home to make myself some dinner and watch BMX videos.

• Where do you see yourself in the next 10 years and what are your aspirations outside of your BMX career?

I honestly don't see myself that far ahead. I can't say I only focus on the now but I do think about how to be better tomorrow than I was today. I currently don't have any aspirations outside of BMX. I'm taking things day by day for now. Ultimately I want to keep striving to be a phenomenal father to my kids.

What trick took you the longest and most effort to master?

That's a hard question. Haha, I don't feel that I've mastered any trick, to be honest. I always keep the mindset that there's always room to improve on anything that I think I'm good at.

-Describe your experiences with previous sponsors as opposed to now?

I've learned a lot from past sponsors. And those experiences showed me how to be transparent and honest about what I want out of a brand, what I can offer the brand, and what we can achieve together.

• How has this pandemic helped you work on your craft?

It's honestly been super helpful. Riding and also filming comes with a lot; from dealing with random people, security, and cops. Businesses being closed means there are fewer people around to hassle you for riding. I've been able to consistently ride way more spots than before.

NIGEL
SYLVESTER

Nigel Sylvester, 33, has made a name for himself in the BMX scene. He is known for his trendsetting style, entertaining content, and impressive tricks . The Queens native has garnered over 80 million viewers on Youtube and is known for his live action videos through New York City streets. His visuals are reminiscent of video games — almost like GTA but for BMX— with nothing but a GoPro and his witty commentary we watch Sylvester ride through Chinatown simultaneously performing tricks and avoiding moving vehicles.

Sylvester is glad to call Laurelton, Queens, his home. "Queens is one of the most diverse places in the world, so while I was out riding on the daily, I was exposed to a good deal of everything; those experiences help me quickly understand what I wanted out of life," said Sylvester.

With his daredevil shenanigans, Sylvester continues to break barriers and create new, quirky content for the world to see. PREME Magazine had the opportunity to sit down with the Nike athlete and discuss what it means to him to be one of the pioneers of BMX and an inspiration to his community.

How did you get introduced to Bike riding?

I got introduced to BMX in my neighborhood. I grew up watching my older cousins and different kids in my hood pull up on the latest BMX bikes, pop wheelies, and do bunnyhops. From that moment I was hooked, I knew I wanted to have a nice bike and do tricks. As I got older, I discovered athletes around the world who rode BMX bikes professionally as a career, and that's when the dream of becoming a Professional BMX athlete was born. I dedicated all my time and energy to perfecting my craft. My focus was to be the best. I undoubtedly believed that if I put my all into riding, I would achieve success.

His professional dedication to BMX helped him land a major endorsement deal with Nike in 2003, this was a huge accomplishment for Sylvester having been a huge fan of Nike brand growing up

What does it mean to you to be a Nike Athlete?

I signed with Nike shortly after turning pro. I was 18 years old and just dropped out of college to pursue my BMX career full time. At that moment, it was surreal, and at times it still feels that way. I grew up buying Nike sneakers from the different sneakers spots on the colosseum block, idealizing Nike athletes like MJ, Deion, Penny, Tiger, and watching those classic Nike commercials on TV. Having the opportunity to join the family and make my own history

From Jay-Z shoutouts to performing eye-catching bike tricks in A$AP Ferg music video, Sylvester is a familiar face in the hip hop scene as well. Indeed, music means everything to Nigel, and we took a peek at Nigel's riding playlist and "[he's] got Hov, Meek, Da Baby, Florence & The Machine, Money Man, Brent Faiyaz, Ross, Ella Mai, Drake, N.E.R.D, ASAP, to name a few," lists Sylvester.

As a BMX Rider, expressing oneself through tricks, music, and riding style is foundational to one's brand. But of course, a sense of fashion helps; Sylvester considers himself a sneakerhead, and his go-to shoe is the Air Jordan 1. "Beyond it being my favorite pair of sneakers to ride in, it's my ultimate life shoe. I can literally everything in the AJ1," says Sylvester. Moreover, he was one of the first BMX riders to launch his very own signature Air Jordan 1 back in 2018.

3. Your fluidity on your bike, fashion, and music choice in your videos give an unmatched denomination. Describe your creative process when coming up with content for your fans?

My creative process is like a flowing river. I'm always thinking about new ideas, and I draw inspiration from a multitude of places. Whether it's making a video or a film, perfecting a product, or figuring out a moment. I love creating; it fuels me, from the inception point of an idea, to the work that goes into producing it and sharing the final product with my fans and community. I find pleasure and purpose in the entire process.

4. You are an inspiration to many Black BMX riders. Who did you admire while coming up into the BMX industry?

Coming up in the BMX industry, I admired the greats, the riders who contributed new ways to look at BMX, and the ones who changed the game. Dave Mirra, Edwin Delarosa, Bob Haro, those guys are legends. They did tricks and made power moves during their career that shifted BMX culture forever. They inspired me to ride at the highest levels and approach the business side of being a professional athlete with the same intensity.

5. What would you like to change in the BMX industry regarding diversity?

I want to see the BMX industry use more of an open mind when it comes to BMX athletes furthering their careers and growing their brands. I want to see BMX companies provide their riders with more opportunities within the BMX industry and outside the industry to make money and support themselves. I got ridiculed by various enthusiasts and media outlets within the BMX industry for doing things in a non-tradition BMX manner throughout my career. Still, those same moves allowed me to grow and expand my brand beyond the "BMX norms" creating career-changing opportunities for me to express myself.

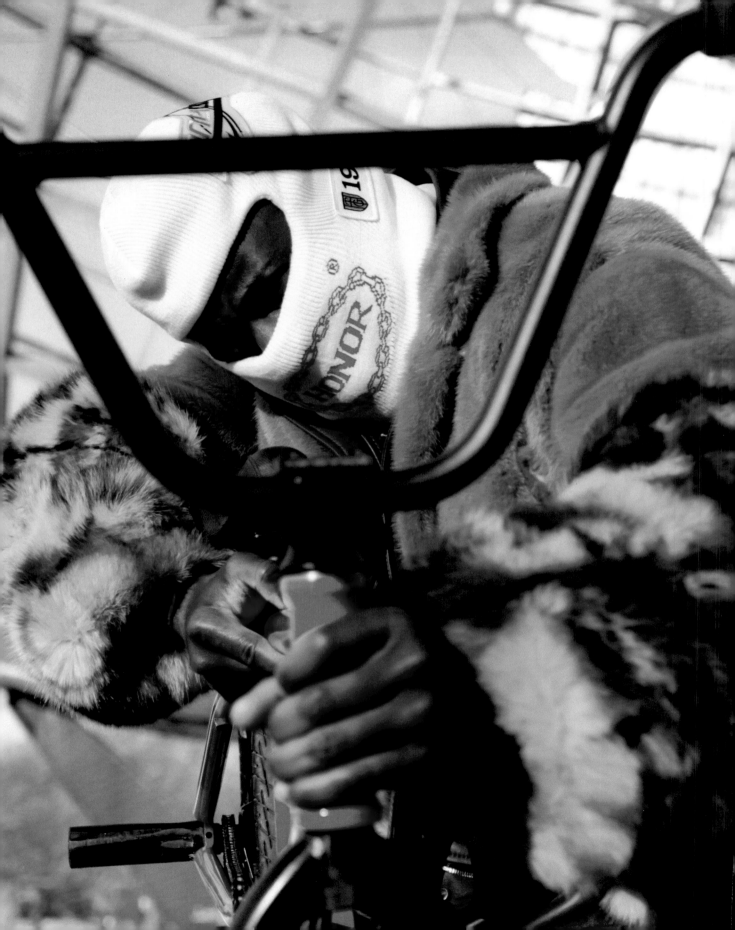

Sylvester strives to break the stigma around BMX Riding. With BMX being a predominantly white sport, many Black kids don't see it as a legitimate career path. He prioritizes using his platform to educate young Black kids from all walks of life about BMX.

How do you use platforms to give back to your community?
I use my platform as a conduit to connect with kids and communities in need. I work with a couple of non-for-profit organizations, Life Camp and Cycle Kids, together, we've supported communities in need with access to bicycles and various resources. I'm also a leading member of a bicycle organization called Bike Rides For Black Lives. Our goal is to support our communities through bicycling by using it as a form of mental/ physical therapy and a tool to rally around important issues.

As a reputable athlete and man, Sylvester is set on becoming one of the best BMX riders of his generation. He continues to better himself on and off the bike. Not only as a rider, but also as a leader in his community, giving back, inspiring, and educating young Black athletes.